DEDICATION

We have been richly blessed by wonderful people who
have inspired us to live life to its fullest in every way.
Thank you.

INTRODUCTION

Throw this handy guide in your car and choose your own
Cache Valley adventure. Open randomly to any page and
go. There are activities for everyone. Use it for dates, family
adventures or for heading out on your own. It might be fun
to write the date and even a few notes about your escapades
on each entry. We roll our eyes when locals say there's
nothing to do around here. Hopefully these suggestions
will change your mind. We know there are thousands of
additional things to do, people to meet and food to taste, and
we hope these ideas will inspire you to discover the beauty
and experiences that already surround you. Enjoy!

OUTDOORS

Fishing at First Dam

1

DISCOVER
THE BEST VIEW OF THE VALLEY

The first eye-popping view locals think of is heading north into the valley on Hwy. 89. Drive around the final bend and Cache Valley's expanse becomes an impressive panorama. A grand adventure is to go exploring and find your own best views. In the meantime, a few of our additional favorites are:

1099 Mountain Road in Logan (head east on Center Street and keep left. It turns into Mountain Road and in a few blocks you'll see a random ironwork park bench on the left.

On Temple Hill in Logan, there's a park bench on the corner of the Boulevard and 100 North. You can see the entire south end of the valley.

5131 West Hwy. 30 in Benson. Head west on Hwy. 30 (200 North) for about 7 miles from Main Street in Logan. Get ready to dive off the road on the left-hand side. There's a pull-out area where you can view the valley west to the Bear River Range and you're practically sitting at the base of the Wellsville Mountains to the east. *Tip:* Bring a camp chair and binoculars if you have them. The area is full of birds. Relax and enjoy.

2

HIKE BY THE LIGHT OF THE
SILVERY MOON

The steep 2-mile hike to the Wind Caves is definitely worth it for the view. You can see China Wall, a solid limestone formation that runs up and down this section of Logan Canyon. You'll climb above a triple arch that looks a lot like nostrils from the parking lot below. The Wind Caves are also known as Witch's Castle, and some prefer to hike the trail by the light of a full moon. If you're not that coordinated with the moon and a flashlight, hike in the earlier morning hours because it can get super hot in the afternoon.

 5 miles up Logan Canyon
Milepost 466.4

 No phone

 No website

3

MOUNTAINOUS BEAUTY
AND FRESH AIR

Take advantage of two ways to explore the vistas and valleys of the Bear River mountain range. Mosey on up to Beaver Creek Lodge from June through mid-October to mount a trusty steed (in case you're not a cowboy, that means horse) to take a trail ride. Your guide will lead you through breathtaking scenery. Don't worry, the horses are very tame and used to clueless riders. We can vouch for that.

If you like four wheels better than four legs, rent a side-by-side RZR (pronounced "razor"). It's basically a squatty jeep convertible without windows. We thought we'd be chiropractic disasters, but they have great shocks. The friendly folks at the Lodge give you a map and suggestions for your ride. One poignant destination is the monument to 37 Korean soldiers who were killed when their plane crashed in Logan Canyon in 1953. RZRs seat 4-6 people and give you the flexibility to head off-road comfortably. You'll spy wildflowers, wildlife, beaver lodges, lakes and who knows what else.

 26 miles up Logan Canyon
Milepost 486.8

 (435) 753-1076

 beavercreeklodge.com

4

PICNIC AND
PLAY AT THE PARK

Our towns are full of tree-lined, shady parks. Visiting is an enjoyable way to catch some sunshine or some shade, depending on what you want. There's plenty of space for kids to run amok and picnic tables to lay out your spread. A few of our favorites are:

Ryan's Place Park: 400 South 600 East in River Heights; not shady but is designed to be handicap accessible and has great playground equipment.

Adams Park: 550 North 500 East in Logan; includes playground and sand volleyball pits.

Mack Park: 70 Canyon Rd. in Smithfield • (435) 563-0048; horseshoe pits, fire pit, volleyball area, covered picnic tables and one of the best spots for family photos in the valley.

5

VISIT
PORCUPINE RESERVOIR

We love to take the scenic drive to Porcupine at the south end of the valley. The ride is as beautiful as the destination. The towns are small and there are lots of fields with a variety of crops. You can also view the Wellsville Mountains from a different perspective. Head past Avon on Hwy. 165 and turn left on Canyon Road. We usually see deer along the way. The dam itself is earthen and was built in 1964. There's a fairly extensive shoreline and the fishing is good. Keep in mind that once you venture past the wall of the dam, it's an unimproved dirt road. During late August through mid-September bright orange kokanee salmon will be spawning and heading upriver from the dam. We haven't seen their annual procession, but we hear it's quite the sight.

 See general directions above and/or get a map

 No phone

 No website

6

SLEDS FOR GROWNUPS

Winter junkies know that "deep POW" means "deep powder" and we've got plenty of it. Snowmobiling up Logan Canyon is consistently ranked in the top 10 in the nation and you can get your fill by renting a snowmobile (aka sled) at Beaver Creek Lodge. Take off on a guided tour or an adventure on your own through a sparkling winter wonderland. "But wait! I have no mittens warm enough," you say. Fear not! They'll bundle you up from head to toe in the newest, warmest, classiest winterwear.

 26 miles up Logan Canyon
Milepost 486.8

 (435) 753-1076

 beavercreeklodge.com

11

BECOME A
GLUTTON
FOR PUNISHMENT

Cache Valley has become a haven for really impressive sporting events. Start training now to run in the Wasatch Back Relay, a 24-hour run through the mountains from Logan to Park City; Top of Utah half or full marathon or the Bear 100 where runners lope through cross-country terrain for 100 miles. In a row. Without stopping. If you'd rather test your metal with the pedal, Cache Valley sports Little Red, one of the largest women's-only rides in the nation; the MS150; Gran Fondo and LoToja, short for Logan to Jackson, the longest sanctioned single rider event in the country: 206 miles from Logan to Jackson, Wyoming. These are just a few. If you're more of the I-watch-golf-on-TV-for-exercise person, it's exhilarating to watch these athletes take off from the starting line or make their final finish. Cheer them on for some extra inspiration.

 Various Locations

 (435) 755-1890 (Visitors Bureau)

 explorelogan.com

12

SHOW ME
THE BIRD

If you still think most birds are brown little dots in the sky, it's time to open your eyes to the world of color and variety found in more than 300 species that migrate through Cache Valley. We really want you to see a white-faced Ibis, which is totally misnamed since the bird is entirely dark and iridescent except for the teeniest white outline around its eyeballs. It's actually a really rare bird, but they love Cache Valley. They have a super long, curved beak and long legs. In the air they're so skinny they look like flying pencils. You'll spy them in farmers' fields and in the marshes. Pick up a bird guide and a birding trails brochure at the Visitors Bureau and start looking to the skies.

 Anywhere Outside

 (435) 755-1890 (Visitors Bureau)

 bridgerlandaudubon.org

13

OUTDOORS

SEE THE CROWN JEWEL OF THE
BEAR RIVER MOUNTAINS

Cache Valley residents have been escaping to Tony Grove Lake since the early 1900s when they cranked up their Model Ts and chugged up the canyon. The winding 7-mile drive off Highway 89 is easier now but gives you the same incredible reward: a peaceful getaway to a small lake where you can smell the pine trees and hear the birds. There's a walking path around the lake and it's also the starting point for other hiking trails. By mid-July dozens of varieties of colorful wildflowers will be bursting on the hills. In fall it's colorful leaves instead. In winter you can snowmobile and showshoe. In summer, moose are often seen standing in the lake, unless Julie is with you, in which case you will never see a moose, ever.

 20 miles up Logan Canyon
Milepost 480.8

 (435) 755-3620 (Ranger District)

 explorelogan.com

❧ 14 ❧

SLEIGH BELLS RING

One of the dreamiest wintertime Cache Valley experiences is taking a horse-drawn sleigh or wagon ride through the huge herd of elk at Hardware Ranch Elk Refuge. You'll get to see up to 600 huge bulls and cows up close as they lounge about and munch on hay provided for them. Informative drivers teach you about the majestic animals while you're stopped in the middle of the herd. Dress warmly and bring your camera. Did we mention dressing warmly? We bring a blanket to sit on because those wagon benches are mighty chilly. Bring your own snacks and hot chocolate because they usually don't sell concessions. The season runs from December through February as weather permits.

 15 miles east of Hyrum in Blacksmith Fork Canyon

 (435) 753-6168

 hardwareranch.com

❧ 15 ❧

CLIMB EVERY MOUNTAIN
AND THIS TIME BRING THE KIDS

Bring along your oxygen or be prepared to take things a little slower when you hike the Limber Pine Nature Trail at an altitude of 7,800 feet. The mile-long trail gains 180 feet, so it's actually pretty gradual (thankfully). The trail is named for five separate limber pine trees that have grown together for more than 550 years. The loop trail has some informative interpretive signs, which is great for teaching kids (and yourself, for that matter). Look forward to the glimpses you'll get of Bear Lake in the distance.

31 miles up Logan Canyon
Milepost 419.9

(435) 755-3620 (Ranger District)

No website

⁓ 16 ⁓

ZIPPITY DOO DAH
GO VISIT ZOOTAH

Our well-kept zoo (formerly known as Willow Park) is the ideal size for families. There are about 80 species of animals, reptiles and birds. A few of our favorite mammals to see are the monkeys, hedgehog, bobcat, porcupines and yak (mostly because saying "yak" makes Julie laugh out loud). There are eagles and owls and cranes, as well brilliantly colored macaws and other tropical birds. The Zootah website has a link to worksheets kids can use to learn more while they're there.

 419 West 700 South in Logan

 (435) 750-9894

 willowparkzoo.wixite.com

17

ROW, ROW, ROW
YOUR BOAT

It's so peaceful to paddle a canoe through the Cutler Wetlands. This maze takes you through an array of habitats like cattails or marshes, so you get to see a variety of birds and sometimes wildlife. You're not that far from the highway, but you're in a whole different world. Download a map at <u>BridgerlandAudubon.org/WetlandsMaze</u>. To rent canoes on the edge of the water so you don't have to haul them yourself, call Muddy Road Outfitters. Jim and Barbara are super nice and they know everything about the features of the area. They can accommodate groups of all sizes and they also have a firepit and plenty of room to play. *Tips:* Don't forget to wear bug repellant and sunscreen. You might want to bring some water and snacks.

 4705 West 3800 North in Benson

 (435) 753-3693

 muddyroad.net

❧ 18 ❧

FORE!

Cache Valley has some outstanding and affordable golf courses. First, Logan River, an 18-hole, Par 71 course, which means nothing to us because we don't golf. What *does* mean something to us is the Logan River winds through it, so you can see birds and enjoy the trees and scenery too. You can also hit a bucket of balls on the driving range, which is fun even when you have no idea what you're doing. Head north to Smithfield's Birch Creek course for another 18 holes and impressive views of the mountains. Even if you've never golfed, the scenery alone might be enough to inspire you to start.

Logan River: 550 West 1000 South in Logan
(435) 750-0123 • loganutah.org

Birch Creek: 550 East 100 North in Smithfield
(435) 563-6825 • birchcreekgolf.com

19

THE LAST
UNSPOILED PLACE

A National Geographic author titled Logan Canyon National Scenic Byway the last unspoiled place, and it certainly must be one of them. We're so fortunate that Logan Canyon is uncommercialized because the entire length of it is full of opportunities for hiking, biking, fishing, camping, snowmobiling, skiing and snowshoeing. You can also birdwatch, look for fossils, practice your geology identification skills, geocache, picnic, rock climb, photograph or simply fill your lungs with the pine- and aspen-scented mountain air. Any time is a great time to take a drive (although winter can be a bit nerve-racking if you're a chicken like Jesse) on the 43-mile road between Logan and Bear Lake.

 Hwy. 89 from Logan to Bear Lake

 (435) 755-3620 (Ranger District)

 explorelogan.com (download Logan Canyon brochure)

20

GET AWAY TO
HYRUM STATE PARK

We enjoy visiting Hyrum State Park because it's less crowded than most places and has plenty of room to spread out on the banks and beach of the reservoir. You'll find a nicely maintained campground and a great group area with a big firepit for making smores or holding a fireside. It's a fun place for boating, waterskiing, swimming, standup paddle boarding, relaxing in the sun and fishing. You might even go home with a trophy bass, trout, perch or bluegill.

 405 West 300 South in Hyrum

 (435) 245-6866

 stateparks.utah.gov/parks/hyrum

❧ 21 ❧

DAM, DAM, DAM

Apparently Loganites were not that creative when they titled some of the locations up the canyon, as evidenced by the names First Dam, Second Dam and Third Dam. Call them what you will, but they are all great places for a picnic or a walk and the incredible component we take for granted is that First Dam is only 1 mile away from the city. In 5 minutes you can get from downtown to the national forest. Awesome! We like to snag sack lunches from the Old Grist Mill (their sugar cookies are the best) or Great Harvest and head up the canyon. You'll find lots of families, swimmers, paddleboarders and volleyball players at First Dam. Second Dam is handicap accessible and there are several firepits along the water. Third Dam is marshy and has lots of willows. Several trails, including the popular Crimson Trail, start here. Any of the dams is a great spot for a quick getaway.

 1-4.2 miles up Logan Canyon
Mileposts 462.4, 463.7 and 465.5

 (435) 755-3620 (Ranger District)

 explorelogan.com (download Logan Canyon brochure)

22

SEE A
SPECTACULAR SUNSET

One of our all-time favorite places to be overwhelmed by a colorful Cache Valley sunset is the Lower Bear River Outlook in Benson. There are regal pelicans diving into the water or just bobbing along with other birds too. Fish are jumping out of the smooth water and it's so quiet you can hear the bugs fly. The sky turns brilliant shades of yellow, orange and red while you watch with wonder.

 3853 North 3800 West in Benson

 No phone

 No website

23

HOOK, LINE AND SINKER

This is our kind of fishing. You don't have to have a license and at Mountain Valley Trout the fish are basically floating around waiting for you to toss them a snack on a hook. The farm raises about 100,000 trout every year and you can catch rainbows, browns and tigers. Some like to catch and release, but we're too wimpy for that because we'd actually have to touch the fish and pull the hook out. Others catch to keep, and the staff is happy to clean and fillet the fish. If you only want to eat the trout without doing any of the work, let them know and they'll net them and fillet them for you.

 1471 West Hwy. 281 in Smithfield

 (435) 563-3647

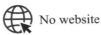 No website

24

THOSE ARE SOME
DEEP ROOTS

Honestly, we've never hiked the Old Juniper Trail. It's 11 miles roundtrip, but hikers and mountain bikers are rewarded with views of the Bear River Range, wildflowers in spring and bright-colored leaves in fall. The goal, of course, is to see the Jardine Juniper tree, which is estimated to be over 1,500 years old. You can't really miss it since it's 26 feet 8 inches in circumference and 44 feet 6 inches tall. Old Juniper was discovered in 1923, and is one of the largest juniper trees in the world.

 10 miles up Logan Canyon
Milepost 471.6

 (435) 755-3620 (Ranger District)

 explorelogan.com
(download hiking brochure)

25

GET BACK TO
NATURE

Stokes Nature Center is a year-round trove of information and experiential activities for all ages. Learn about the landscape, wildlife and geology of Logan Canyon. Hit one of their popular Canyon Jams outdoor concerts during the summer months. Stokes has teamed up with Bridger Folk Music Society for lively tunes in the open air. Stokes hosts other activities like snowshoeing treks in the winter. Check their website for hours and events.

 1 mile up Logan Canyon
Milepost 463

 (435) 755-3239

 logannature.org

✌ 26 ✌

LOOK BUT
DON'T DRINK

Sixteen miles up Logan Canyon you'll spy Ricks Spring on the left. Park and carefully cross the road to investigate the rock cavern gushing with cold spring water. Generations of travelers have stopped to fill their jugs, but turns out it's not your best idea anymore. Scientists figured out some of the Logan River flows into the spring so it's contaminated with Giardia, a little organism that will give you intestinal woe you won't soon forget. It's worth the stop, though. It's pretty and you can take some cool photos.

 16 miles up Logan Canyon
Milepost 476.9

 (435) 755-3620 (Ranger District)

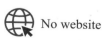 No website

27

HIT THE SLOPES

We love Beaver Mountain. Here's a little trivia for you: It's the longest running family-owned ski resort in the nation and the Seeholzers have been doing it right since 1939. Skiing or boarding the Beav is a completely different experience compared to the high-falutin' resorts down south. The rates are more affordable, and everyone is friendly. You feel like family even if you're complete strangers. The Beav has 4 lifts and 48 runs so there's plenty of room to spread out. We love the fact that year-round their voicemail always ends "Pray for snow!"

 27 miles up Logan Canyon

 (435) 946-3610

 skithebeav.com

28

ON TOP
OF THE WORLD

If you are in extraordinarily good shape and a little bit crazy, conquer the peaks of the Wellsvilles along the Wellsville Ridge. It's a bucket list item for many, but be prepared. Take a lot of water and food. The highest elevation tops out at more than 9,300 feet and the Wellsvilles are the steepest mountains in the world. Not the tallest, but the steepest from base to peak and you'll feel it. The views of Cache Valley to the east and Box Elder County, including the Great Salt Lake, to the west are jaw-droppingly gorgeous. You'll probably see lots of birds of prey from late August through mid-November. Any time you go, you will likely encounter mosquitos and biting flies, sections of overgrown trail and not much shade.

 Wellsville to Mendon

 No phone

 Search for trail maps online

❧ 29 ❧

GET LOST

Each fall people flock in droves to Cache Valley corn mazes. The dried stalks are as high as an elephant's eye and pathways have been mowed into acres and acres. The mazes would be easy to navigate from the air since you could easily see the patterns, which are unique images with confusing twists and turns inside to throw you off. If you are directionally challenged, wandering around lost will be nothing new. We have two mazes in the valley. First, the American West Heritage Center where they also have a pumpkin patch, a bounce house, games, a straw fort and a haunted hollow on the weekends. Second, Little Bear Bottoms, which also features a lengthy spook alley, a spooky wagon ride and the haunted river trail. *Tip:* Dress warmer than you think you need to and remember to bring some gloves.

AWHC: 4025 South Hwy. 89-91 in Wellsville
(435) 245-6050 • awhc.org

Little Bear Bottoms: 5000 South Hwy. 89-91 in Wellsville
(435) 770-3462 or (435) 770-5273 • lbbcornmaze.com

❧ 30 ❧

GO FISH

Fly-fishing enthusiasts love the Logan River, a blue-ribbon trout stream recognized as one of the best in the region. The lower dams in the canyon are stocked with brown and rainbow trout. Farther up the canyon you can catch plenty of cutthroat trout. There's also great fishing on the Blacksmith Fork near Hyrum, at Hyrum State Park, Newton Dam and over the hill in Bear Lake.

 Anywhere fish hang out

 (435) 755-3620 (Ranger District)

 explorelogan.com (download fishing brochure)

❧ **31** ❧

JUST DIVE IN

The Logan Aquatic Center has two pristine pools for swimming and soaking up the sun. The large leisure pool for kids has fun water features for them to play in. The big pool has two fast slippery slides and a low and high diving board—the site of one of Julie's most embarrassing moments. That's another story for another day. The Aquatic Center is a great spot for family fun or for swimming laps all summer long.

 415 South 500 West in Logan

 (435) 716-9266

 loganutah.org

32

PUTT PUTT

We love to play 18 holes—of miniature golf, that is. The Willows is great for anyone at any skill level, especially if you're just there to have fun. Jesse makes a birdie or an eagle or a flamingo or some other kind of fowl on every hole because he has no idea what he's doing or how to keep score. We enjoy early evenings best, but you'll have a blast whenever you go. They also have a picnic spot and they usually give you a Popsicle when you finish.

 220 Spring Creek in Providence

 (435) 752-4255

 willowsgolfpark.com

❧ 33 ❧

SKIING & BOARDING & TUBING, OH MY!

Cherry Peak is the newest ski resort in Utah. In addition to skiing and snowboarding, you can fly down a 580-foot-long tubing hill. The best part? They have a moving sidewalk so when we go it can haul our sorry carcasses to the top. Rent your tubes there and hold on for dear life. In the summer you can take in outdoor concerts, mountain biking, disc golf, bungee jumping, horseback riding and other activities.

 3200 East 11000 North in Richmond

 (435) 200-5050

 skicherrypeak.com

UTAH'S HEART OF THE ARTS

Utah Festival Opera and Musical Theatre

34

TAKE THE STAGE

When you walk inside the 1923 Ellen Eccles Theatre your mouth will fall open. It's inconceivable that a theater this ornate could possibly be found in a community our size. It seats 1,093 and there are more than 300 days of performances every year. You automatically feel classy and important when you walk up the promenade with its carved alcoves and beautiful paintings to get into the house (actual theater). The décor is full of symbolism. On the left you'll see a giant mural depicting the legend of the Phoenix. The bird is crashing down into flames, a reference to the Thatcher Opera House that went up in smoke in 1912. On the right is the Phoenix being resurrected more beautiful and resplendent than before, just like the new 1923 theater was. Above the stage, notice the face of a Greek muse showering down blessings of peace and artistic inspiration on the audience and performers. *Tips:* 1. Walk to the front, turn around and admire the entire gem. 2. The seats begin to rise on Row H, so you get a 1-inch boost above the poofy hair in front of you.

 43 South Main in Logan

 (435) 752-0026

 centerforthearts.us

✦ **35** ✦

STROLL AROUND
SUMMERFEST
ARTS FAIRE

Summerfest Arts Faire has a super cool vibe and is Logan's kickoff for summer. You'll meander past the wares of more than 150 artists (they're juried in, which means they have to be really good and pretty unique), catch live music of all sorts and drool over dozens of food booths. Think of doing your Christmas shopping early—handmade original paintings, jewelry, ceramics, sculptures, yard art and more. It's always held the Thursday through Saturday of Father's Day weekend on the shady grounds of the Tabernacle.

 50 North Main in Logan

 (435) 213-3858

 logansummerfest.com

UTAH FESTIVAL

We can hardly wait for the opening week of Utah Festival Opera and Musical Theatre's performances every summer. Hundreds of talented performers audition, and the very best are selected to move here for a couple months while they rehearse and perform. They have played roles in little places you might have heard of like Broadway and the Metropolitan Opera, plus every other prestigious stage there is. Utah Festival presents four huge shows like *Mary Poppins, The Marriage of Figaro* and *West Side Story* in repertory with full orchestra, which is a big deal because you can rarely find a full orchestra accompaniment anywhere these days. This is how performances are meant to be done. They surround the shows with other great events like interactive hourlong classes as part of the Festival Academy (think learning how to speak with an accent, an introduction to choreography or how to stage fight). There are backstage tours, breakfast with the stars on Saturday mornings, a gala dinner, black and white films accompanied by a Mighty Wurlitzer Organ, lectures and more. Utah Festival crams more than 150 events into their 5-week season July through the first week of August and we wish we could attend every one.

 43 South Main in Logan

 (435) 750-0300 ext. 3

 utahfestival.org

THE ARTS

37

UTAH STATE'S
SCULPTURE WALK

This is SO cool. Utah State University has 35 sculptures across campus and the Nora Eccles Harrison Museum has created three walking tours of different lengths to help you see all of them. The subjects range from regional and national history to colorful mosaics to what-in-the-world-is-this? (Surely only our unsophisticated art-viewing brains would wonder such a thing.) Two of our favorites are *Synergy* and *Untitled Mosaic*. The walking tour info is optimized for your phone and even contains audio tours. It's a great way to explore campus, especially after 5 p.m. or on weekends when you can park almost anywhere without a pass.

 650 North 1100 East, USU campus

 (435) 797-0163 (Museum)

 artmuseum.usu.edu

38

ALL THE
BELLS & WHISTLES

The Utah Theatre opened as the Roxy in the 1930s and recently reopened after a decade-long $11 million renovation and expansion to take it back to its early Art Deco splendor. The place is also home to a donated $1 million Mighty Wurlitzer Theatre Organ. Only 100 of them remain in the United States. This is the gigantic organ you imagine with three consoles (keyboards) and hundreds of buttons that trigger an entire room full of instruments including drums, pipes, bells and whistles. Normal people can't even play the thing. You have to be a professional movie theatre organist to make it really sing. For a very rare experience, go to one of their silent black and white films. The organist sits on the bench and presents the entire accompaniment while he's watching it too. Unbelievable. Do. Not. Miss. It. Meanwhile, catch a classic film or even a singalong almost every night Monday-Saturday. Live performances are held during the summer. *Tip:* The chandeliers inside are duplicates of those in the Metropolitan Opera and the 2-story chandelier in the lobby is Swarovski crystal.

 18 West Center in Logan

 (435) 750-0300 ext. 3

 theutahtheatre.com

✺ **39** ✺

ART LOVERS UNITE

One of our favorite ways to spend a Friday evening is walking around historic downtown Logan and ducking our heads inside galleries and businesses that become galleries for the quarterly Gallery Walk. Different spots have live music and/or refreshments, and you're bound to find cool people and amazing art. Local artists from beginners to beyond professional showcase oil and watercolor paintings, sculpture, pottery, photography and jewelry. More than a dozen renowned artists live in Cache Valley, but it's tough to find their work here because they're too busy filling galleries in places like Jackson, Wyoming; Carmel, California and New York City. Nevertheless, here are a few of our favorite galleries we frequent year-round.

Logan Fine Art
60 West 100 North in Logan • (435) 753-0333
loganfineartgallery.com

Fuhrimans Framing and Fine Art
75 South Main in Logan • (435) 752-0370 • Facebook

Prince Art Gallery
2600 North Main #106 in North Logan • (435) 750-6089
princegallerylogan.com

40

SEE A
SHOW OR TWO
OR HOW ABOUT FOUR?

There is no question. You must go to the Lyric Rep performances held each summer mid-June through mid-August in the 1913 Caine Lyric Theatre. The Lyric Rep is one of the only true remaining repertory companies in the nation. That means the same lead performers star in a rotating schedule featuring a musical, a mystery, a drama and a comedy. You should see at least one of their performances, but the true magic happens when you see all four. It's mindboggling to watch the performers stretch their skills in the different genres. Ask yourself if you could play the bad guy in a murder mystery one afternoon, then fall down the stairs in a slapstick comedy that evening. The theatre itself is a showstopper. It seats just under 400 and there's not a bad seat in the house. *Tip:* Take a look at the Austria-Hungarian coat of arms (the yellow and black one) on the left side of the stage. At the bottom you can see some broken chunks. That happened decades ago when a patriotic attendee full of anti-German sentiment ran up and hacked it with an ax. And yes, they have a ghost.

 28 West Center in Logan

 (435) 797-8022

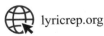 lyricrep.org

VIEW ONE OF THE MOST IMPRESSIVE
COLLECTIONS OF
UTAH ART
IN THE STATE

In the 1930s Cache Valley elementary students donated their milk money (5-10 cents each) to purchase original works of art to decorate their schools. Many of the artists later became regionally and nationally well-known: LeConte Stewart, James Harwood and Minerva Teichert are a few. The Cache County School District eventually pulled the artwork out of the schools and put the paintings in the district offices. This incredible collection represents one of the largest repositories of work by Utah artists in the state. They are all on display and you can see them any time during normal business hours.

 2063 North 1200 East in North Logan

 435-792-7600

 No website

42

MUSIC, MUSIC, MUSIC

We can't think of anywhere else that provides a free concert every single weekday for two-and-a-half months. The popular Noon Music at the Tabernacle series presents a variety of talented performers. You'll hear anything from barbershop to flutes to harps to banjo to the huge pipe organ to…it's different daily and consistently fantastic. Mondays always feature professional musicians who are in town to perform with Utah Festival Opera and Musical Theatre. These concerts run from mid-May through July and last about 45 minutes. They are held in the 1891 Tabernacle, a beautiful example of early Mormon pioneer architecture.

 50 North Main in Logan

 No phone

 logantabernacle.blogspot.com

43

EXPAND YOUR
ART APPRECIATION

Step right in to one of the most extensive collections of modern and contemporary art created in the Western United States during the last century. That's just the beginning. The Nora Eccles Harrison Museum of Art collection contains more than 5,000 pieces of art of all kinds made by 1,845 artists. No, we haven't seen all of them, but we're going to try. The museum completed a major renovation in 2018 and added Noni's Café and a museum gift shop where you can pick up ceramics, jewelry and other art pieces created by USU alums and artists around the state. Take advantage of their monthly Community Art Day, guided tours and lectures. You'll also see their mobile art truck cruising around to educate and provide art opportunities at a variety of locations.

 650 North 1100 East, USU campus

 (435) 797-0163

 artmuseum.usu.edu

44

WE JUST CAN'T GET ENOUGH
GREAT THEATRE AND MUSIC

This valley has an absolutely ridiculous number of musically and artistically talented residents. Maybe it comes from our pioneer heritage who had nothing else to do in the winter besides freeze to death or dance, sing, perform or learn to play an instrument. Maybe it's the following generations of mean mothers who forced their kids to practice, practice, practice until they became virtuosos. Whatever it is, we're totally lucky because we have several amazing choirs and three amazing theater companies that produce shows using local talent that give national productions a run for their money. For real. Some even have live orchestra accompaniment. Catch a performance by any of them and you'll definitely be impressed.

American Festival Chorus • americanfestivalchorus.org

USU's Caine College of the Arts • cca.usu.edu
See anything you can in the Daines Concert Hall on campus. It was exquisitely renovated in 2018 and has wonderful acoustics.

Cache Theatre • cachetheatre.com

Music Theatre West • musictheatrewest.org

Four Seasons Theatre • fourseasonstheatre.org

HERITAGE

American West Heritage Center

45

THE CENTER
OF IT ALL

The Cache County courthouse was built in 1883 and restored in fine fashion in 2005. It's home of the Cache Valley Visitors Bureau and their awesome team who are more than happy to tell you where to go. If you're new to the area or think you've seen it all, come visit and they'll change your mind. There is an abundance of information and a great gift shop where you can find local products and Logan and Cache Valley gear like shirts, hats, magnets, maps, hiking guides, cow socks and postcards. One of our favorite features in the building is the hand-painted safe that weighs 4,800 pounds and had to be hauled out the window with a crane during the renovation. Open the heavy steel doors and you can literally smell the musty past from the carpet lining the interior.

 199 North Main in Logan

 (435) 755-1890

 explorelogan.com

46

STEP BACK
IN TIME

You really can't imagine how awesome the American West Heritage Center is until you experience it. If it's been awhile, go back because it gets bigger and better all the time. Imagine hundreds of acres of undeveloped farmland and an unobstructed view of the Wellsville Mountains. Then start at the Welcome Center and cross the bridge into a different century: 1820-1920. They even have a small herd of bison. This outdoor living history museum is overflowing with interactive opportunities to explore the Old West hands-on. You can visit with mountain men, pioneers and turn-of-the-century farmers dressed in period costume. Throw hatchets or learn to set traps with the mountain men; make rag dolls or compete in a two-man log-sawing contest on the pioneer site; see the women cooking over a wood-burning stove, watch the blacksmith at work or even learn to milk a cow on the farm. Julie would like to apologize to the poor bovine she bothered.

 4025 South Hwy. 89-91 in Wellsville

 (435) 245-6050

 awhc.org

47

DOWN TO THE
BEAR BONES

In the early 1900s Old Ephraim was a legendary grizzly bear who roamed the Cache National Forest eating fluffy sheep for snacks. Sheepherder Frank Clark had enough when he counted 150 dead sheep in the summer of 1911. He swore vengeance against the 9-foot, 11-inch monster. Old Three Toes (Ephraim's nickname because of a deformity in one paw) was too smart to be caught. He would spring traps set for him with tree stumps or branches. He finally met his demise 12 years later when he and Clark crossed paths in the dark on August 21, 1923. Later, a local troop of Boy Scouts dug up Ephraim's skull and sent it to the Smithsonian Institute where it stayed until 1978 when it was returned and put on display in Special Collections at USU. If you'd like to see the stone monument marking where he was buried, head up Logan Canyon to Right Hand Fork, just past milepost 470. Pick up a good map and a copy of Clark's dramatic (and traumatic) experience at the Visitors Bureau.

 Merrill-Cazier Library on USU Campus

 (435) 797-8148

 archives.usu.edu

48

DISCOVER
HISTORIC
DOWNTOWN

Amble through downtown Logan with its charming cafes, storefronts with character and unique specialty and antique shops. Check out the Mormon pioneer tabernacle, three historic theatres, and the Bluebird, the longest running restaurant in the state. Download or pick up a brochure at the Cache Valley Visitors Bureau so you can learn more about Logan's sometimes-colorful past. For info on downtown events, log on to <u>logandowntown.org.</u>

 199 North Main in Logan

 (435) 755-1890

 explorelogan.com (download brochure)

49

ABOUT THAT TONIC...

Dr. Pierce's barn is a Cache Valley icon. Head a few miles south of Logan to see it and snap some photos. What is this about, you might ask. Well, Dr. Pierce was a crackpot doctor from Buffalo, New York. He invented dozens of remedies in the forms of tonics, pills and elixirs that were guaranteed to cure nearly any ailment. He rented the sides of barns in several states and painted them with advertisements for Dr. Pierce's favorite prescription, his Womans Tonic. According to a 1910 Salt Lake newspaper, the tonic would make "weak women strong, sick women well." After all, "Nine-tenths of all the sickness of women is due to some derangement or disease of the organs distinctly feminine." It either cured you or you didn't care because two of the main ingredients were said to be opium and alcohol. Jesse is still wondering where he can get his hands on some for Julie on occasion.

 4 miles South of Logan on Hwy. 89-91

 No phone

 No website

SHOWCASING
CACHE VALLEY HISTORY

We love the Hyrum Museum. It is very well researched and well organized. One of our favorite exhibits is about the mountain men who frequented this area in the 1820s. The display shows what an actual cache looked like and how supplies were stored inside. Cache Valley got its name from the trappers, who cached (French for hide or store) their furs here. You can also learn about Hyrum's historical heroes, Main Street and a lot more. It's worth the short drive, for sure.

HERITAGE

 50 West Main in Hyrum

 (435) 245-0208

 hyrumcitymuseum.org

51

HONOR
A FLIGHT OF FANCY

Lieutenant Russell Maughan electrified the world when he completed the first dawn to dusk coast to coast flight June 23, 1924. He made the trip from New York to San Francisco and landed one minute before dusk. It was the decorated fighter pilot's third attempt and his feat was heralded in newspapers as a "Maughanumental Achievement." A monument in his honor stands in front of the home where he was born. Take note of the house while you're there because the entire exterior is covered with smooth river rocks.

HERITAGE

 133 East Center in Logan

 No phone

 No website

52

HISTORY WITH A
WORLDWIDE FLAIR

Utah State University's Museum of Anthropology provides a glimpse into worldwide cultures and history. Their varied exhibits include artifacts from Indonesia, Java, Egypt and Peru. The museum incorporates regional history with displays about the prehistoric Great Basin, the Fremont Indians and Chinese railroad camps. Family 1st Saturdays are the best! They are held from 10 a.m.-2 p.m. the first Saturday of every month. All the activities are free, and kids love the arts and crafts. You'll love being exposed to different cultures and themes through food, music, dance and other activities. Check their website for upcoming topics.

 Old Main Room 252 on USU Campus

 (435) 797-7545

 anthromuseum.usu.edu

HERITAGE

53

TWO PROMINENT PIONEERS

Cache Valley is the final resting place of two legendary leaders in the early days of the Church of Jesus Christ of Latter-day Saints.

The Church's first prophet and leader Joseph Smith translated the Book of Mormon from ancient records inscribed on thin plates made of gold. In 1829, three men were allowed to see and touch the plates so they could testify of their legitimacy. The men are known to church members as the Three Witnesses. **Martin Harris** was one of them. He settled and is buried in Mendon. Visit the monument to him in the Clarkston cemetery. On odd-numbered years, community volunteers present a free Church-sponsored outdoor pageant that tells Harris's story.

11000 North 8400 West in Clarkston • clarkstonpageant.org

James Willie was the revered captain of an ill-fated handcart company. He led 501 pioneers in their exodus from Iowa City to Salt Lake City in 1856. Unfortunately, the group left too late in the season and were stranded in unceasing blizzards on the Wyoming plains. Rescuers from Salt Lake City were stunned by the terrible condition of the starving and nearly frozen survivors. The weary crew finally arrived on November 9. Captain Willie settled in Mendon and served as the city's mayor. He is buried in the Mendon cemetery and his rock home is located there too.

25 North 200 West in Mendon • mendonutah.net

54

SKELETONS
IN YOUR CLOSET?

Discover your long-lost relatives at the Family Search Library located downstairs in the Logan Tabernacle. Cheerful volunteers will help you navigate every major genealogy website in existence to fill out your family tree. Somehow all those sites are networked together, and magic detective work happens in a flash. The library is tied in to the largest receptacle of genealogical records in the world, which is owned and managed by the Church of Jesus Christ of Latter-day Saints. All the services are free (except a few cents for printouts) and anyone of any faith or no faith at all can participate. The library provides free classes for those who want to go more in-depth. While you're there, duck your head into the large meeting hall on the main floor. It's a great example of Mormon pioneer architecture. Tours are offered weekdays during the summer and by appointment.

 50 North Main in Logan

 (435) 755-5594

 loganfsl.org

LOGAN'S HOME
SWEET HOMES

The mansions sprinkled along Center Street give you a taste of the lives of Logan's elite at the turn of the century: the Thatchers, Nibleys, Eccles and others. Download or pick up a historic homes brochure at the Visitors Bureau so you can learn more details about the architecture, building methods and their colorful inhabitants. Thirty-three properties are featured. Keep in mind, these are private residences, so don't fling open the front door and walk right in (yes, it has happened).

HERITAGE

 199 North Main (Visitors Bureau)

 (435) 755-1890

 explorelogan.com (download brochure)

WHISPERS
FROM THE PAST

The Logan City Cemetery is a peaceful and shady place, great for a walk and quiet contemplation. The headstones also provide a glimpse into some colorful Cache Valley characters. The Visitors Bureau (199 North Main) has a map of highlights like the Weeping Lady, who supposedly sheds tears over her deceased children during the full moon, a monument to renowned poet Mae Swenson and the Babyland section. Most people take their favorite recipes to the grave, but our favorite marker proclaims one woman's famous fudge recipe engraved on the back.

 1000 North 1200 East in Logan

 (435) 716-9270

 loganutah.org

57

EARLY PIONEERS

The cozy Daughters of the Utah Pioneers Museum is located inside the Cache Valley Chamber of Commerce building, a historical structure that over the decades has served as a post office, court and county clerk's office. The museum has a fine collection of artifacts donated by descendants of Cache Valley pioneers. To give you some idea, there are many beautiful articles of clothing, a sleigh, a hand-carved oxen yoke, fancy handiwork and a cannon. Two of our favorite items are a drum that was used in the Nauvoo Legion and a bed built and carved by Brigham Young, the prophet of the Church of Jesus Christ of Latter-day Saints who led the pioneers on their exodus west.

HERITAGE

 160 North Main in Logan

 (435) 752-5139

 cachedupmuseum.org

YOU'LL BE
BARN AGAIN

Cache Valley's agricultural landscape is dotted with historic barns. A fun way to explore the Valley is to pick up a copy of *Historic Barns of Northern Utah: A Self-Guided Driving Tour* from the Cache Valley Visitors Bureau. It features more than 45 barns in Cache Valley and a dozen more in Box Elder and Rich Counties. The publications share details about construction methods and interesting features about each one.

HERITAGE

 All over Cache Valley

 (435) 755-1890 (Visitors Bureau)

 Search online

NEWTON ROCKS

From the 1870s through the early 1900s, many early settlers of what was then called New Town built their homes from locally quarried rock. It was a vast improvement from their dugouts and cabins that had dirt floors and dirt roofs and often used blankets for the doors and windows. More than a dozen rock homes have been restored and are now private residences. We recommend picking up the 30-page booklet about Newton's history and a history of the homes from the library. They only cost a couple dollars. While you're seeing the sites, stop by the Newton Market, 10 East Main, to investigate an array of merchandise and their little café.

 51 South Center in Newton (Library)

 (435) 563-9283

 pioneerrockhouses.blogspot.com

❧ FOOD ❧

The Bluebird Restaurant

🌀 **60** 🌀

OLÉ!

Café Sabor is a fresh Mexican grill housed in a train station built in 1893. When you walk in, notice the old metal radiator on the left and what was once the ticket window and booth to the right of the gigantic tortilla maker. After that, just focus on the menu. They serve a basket of chips and fresh medium salsa (Julie is a wimp, so it clears her sinuses every time) made in-house as soon as you are seated. You can ask for mild or hot. Pollo Durango, chicken and mushrooms in a creamy tomatillo sauce, is one of their best sellers. We love the tacos al carbon and the sweet pork quesadillas served with sweet pepper jelly.

 600 West Center in Logan

 (435) 752-8088

 cafesabor.com

❧ **61** ❧

WE ALL SCREAM FOR
ICE CREAM

Your life is absolutely incomplete without Aggie Ice Cream. Utah State University has been perfecting the art of making dairy products since the agricultural college was founded in 1888. We both love Aggie Bull Tracks most—chocolate with peanut butter and caramel swirls. Divine! They have 30 flavors and they're all made from milk that comes from cows raised by university students. If you're a local, make it your New Year's resolution to try at least one new flavor.

 750 North 1200 East in Logan

 435-797-2109

 aggieicecream.usu.edu

TASTE LOGAN'S
LIQUID GOLD

Cox Honeyland is buzzing with activity in more ways than one. Step inside their giftshop and you'll be amazed by all the honey and honey products you never knew existed. These fourth-generation beekeepers showcase their 13 flavors of creamed honey (natural honey whipped to keep it from crystallizing), fudge, natural and flavored pure honey, honey butter, honeycomb, pollen collected from local bees that helps with allergies, beeswax candles and delicious honey popcorn (it's like caramel popcorn but with honey instead). That's just a start. You can bring your own container to fill with honey out of their giant tank. A highlight is the beehive behind glass where the bees are making honey and filling the wax cells of their honeycomb.

FOOD

 1780 South Hwy. 89-91 in Logan

 (435) 752-3234

 coxhoney.com

DINE AT
THE OLDEST RESTAURANT
IN UTAH

The iconic Bluebird Restaurant has been serving up specialties like a minced ham sandwich with their secret recipe Neuberger mustard (created by one of its founders) and a teddy-bear sundae since 1914. Twirl around at the soda fountain and try an Iron Port, a regional soda specialty. It's a magical place— we met for the first time on the corner of Center and Main on our way to a singles activity at the Bluebird. A year later we got married and now we're living happily ever after. It just might have been the Bluebird's triple chocolate cake.

FOOD

 19 North Main in Logan

 435-752-3155

 TheBluebirdRestaurant.com

BITE INTO
A CLOUD

There's something dreamy about biting into a fluffy Johnny O's spudnut. Maybe it's the airy texture. Maybe it's the ideal ratio of icing and filling to the donut. Wait, what is a spudnut you might ask? It's a hand-mixed, hand-cut donut delicacy created from potato flour that made its American debut in Utah in the 1940s. Jesse is a fan of the strawberry cake with strawberry icing and Julie says the plain glazed is where it's at. Which one of Johnny O's 27+ types of spudnuts will become your fave?

 630 South Main in Logan

 (435) 227-2155

 johnnyosspudnuts.com

FOOD

HOORAY FOR
FRY SAUCE!

It may be one of the state's only contributions to the culinary world but we're proud of it. Utah's Arctic Circle restaurant invented the American version more than 60 years ago, so by now it's in our blood. We dip fries and onion rings in it, throw it on burgers and whatever else we can think of. Here's the basic version:

1 cup mayonnaise
½ cup ketchup

Sounds easy, but the locals have their own secret variations. You can toss in onion or garlic powder, cayenne pepper for some kick, lemon juice, some portion of barbecue sauce, dill pickle juice, Tabasco, or whatever sounds good. Invent your own. Please don't insult us by saying it's just like Thousand Island salad dressing.

WHERE THE
LOCALS EAT

Angie's Restaurant is the epitome of a great diner. Nearly everything is homemade and dished up in a hurry by friendly servers. The menu is 30 miles long and everything on it is yummy. Jesse promises to try something different, but he loves the breakfast sampler so much he gets it almost every time. Julie fancies the Arizona chicken and all the soups are delicious (especially chicken noodle). Two things you must try: 1. The Kitchen Sink, a gigantic banana split on steroids. Polish it off and get a bumper sticker boasting "I cleaned the sink at Angie's." (One has even been spotted on a safari Jeep in Africa.) 2. A scone—it's not a dry English pastry, it's a regional specialty: deep-fried sweet dough that meets the height of its glory when it's smothered in honey butter.

 690 North Main in Logan

 (435) 752-9252

 angiesrest.com

FOOD

SOMETHING
SMELLS FISHY
AND IT'S NOT WHAT YOU THINK

Enjoy the lovely drive 20 minutes north of Logan to Richmond, home of the PEPPERIDGE Farm factory and outlet store. Our Cache Valley plant bakes those famous cheesy Goldfish Crackers and supplies the entire western United States with the fishy favorite. You can buy umpteen billion fish flavors and about that many types of cookies. You never know what kinds you'll find since it depends on what they've made and what comes in: Milanos, Brussels, Chessmen, gingersnaps, chocolate chip and dozens of others. Everything is discounted, and you can buy seconds in bulk and individual packages of everything else. You should probably bring napkins and a big jug of milk.

 901 North 200 West in Richmond

 (435) 258-2491

 pepperidgefarm.com

❧ 𝟲𝟴 ❧

BURGERS & BEER
ON THE ROOF

The roof of the White Owl Bar is the place to be on any summer afternoon. They grill the burgers right in front of you and there are umbrellas and misting machines to keep you cool. Sip on a cold Big Dog (a tall mug of beer) and while you're at it, try the homemade potato chips.

 36 West Center in Logan

 (435) 753-9165

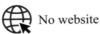 No website

GROUNDS FOR REJOICING

Randy Wirth and Sally Sears started Caffé Ibis more than 40 years ago with a commitment to the environment, to their coffee growers and customers and to exceptional coffee. Ibis was the nation's first company to present triple certified coffee: Organic, Fair Trade and Smithsonian Shade Grown Bird-Friendly. They've been recognized by national magazines and their coffee is custom roasted in batches of 5-190 pounds so every step can be monitored for utmost quality. If coffee isn't your cup of tea (ha!), dive into a cup of Mexicocoa. This rich hot chocolate can't be beat.

FOOD

 52 Federal Ave. in Logan

 (435) 753-4777

 caffeibis.com

70

GARDENERS' MARKET

Head to the historic courthouse square every Saturday from 9 a.m.-1 p.m. mid-May through mid-October for good food, live music, arts and crafts and most importantly: locally grown fruits, vegetables, eggs, meat and fish along with gourmet cheeses, breads and pastries. At the market, all ages and all walks of life are comfortable rubbing shoulders. Sip on lemonade squeezed right before your eyes, get some raspberries or blackberries and pick something you've never tasted from a colorful array of options. Jesse can rarely make it without eating at least one hot chicken tamale and usually tries to buy a dozen to take home when Julie isn't looking.

FOOD

 199 North Main in Logan

 No phone

 gardenersmarket.org

YOU'LL SMILE WHEN YOU
SAY CHEESE

Cache Valley is full of happy cows and you'll be happy too when you try any of Gossner's 30 cheeses. Chances are you already have—they're one of America's largest producers of Swiss cheese and it's served up in restaurants and delis across the country. Head to their retail store for plenty of samples and whatever you do, don't leave without squeaky cheese. Boring businesses might call it cheese curd, but we call it what it is. The cheddar curd squeaks when you chew it before it's chilled and it comes in a variety of flavors. Their shelf-stable boxed milk doesn't have to be refrigerated so you can sip on chocolate, cookies and cream, banana, rootbeer and many others any time.

 1051 North 1000 West in Logan

 (435) 713-6104

 gossner.com

72

AN APPLE
A DAY...

Our mouths are watering just thinking about taking a crunchy bite of a fresh crisp apple straight off the tree from Zollinger Fruit and Tree Farm. Their family has been farming commercially since 1904 and the farmstead is open at least from mid-March to mid-November. If chewing apples sounds like too much effort, you're in luck. Zollingers fresh press a magical blend of 13 varieties of apples to create what is quite possibly the most delightful beverage this side of heaven. You can pick up a gallon at locally owned grocery stores, but nothing beats going straight to the orchard.

FOOD

 1000 River Heights Blvd. in River Heights

 (435) 752-7810

 zollingerfarm.com

73

EVERY DAY SHOULD BE
FRY-DAY

It's getting tough to find fresh-cut French fries these days. Maybe it's too much effort for most, but it's the specialty at Mike's Grill, which is tucked inside the Logan Lanes Bowling Alley. They focus on slices of potato perfection cut on site and dunked quickly in peanut oil then lightly seasoned to ensure total deliciousness. No wonder Yahoo! named them Best Fries in the entire state of Utah. One bite and you'll know why.

 1161 North Main in Logan

 (435) 752-4966

 loganlanesinc.com

74

EAT A FAT BOY
(WHAT?)

No, we don't eat our children. Casper's Ice Cream has been home of the famous giant Fat Boy ice cream sandwich and other delectable frozen delights since 1925. Have a shake or sundae at their fun little Malt Shoppe located near the factory where they crank out 200,000 Fat Boys every day.

 11805 North 200 East in Richmond

 (435) 258-2477

 caspersicecream.com

FOOD

75

HEARTY CHEESE FROM
HARDY COWS

Learn about the craft of artisan cheese-making in a beautiful country setting. Start by saying hello to Rockhill Creamery's six lovely Brown Swiss cows, then head to the underground aging room where handmade wheels of Edam, Gouda, Feta and more ripen to perfection. Take home some of their farmstead cheese along with fresh produce and other items offered at Richmond's Harvest Market held there Saturdays 10 a.m.-1 p.m. June through October. That's when the farmstead is open as well. Not here on a summer Saturday? Get your Rockhill cheese fix at Crumb Brothers Bakery or Gossner Foods.

 563 South State in Richmond

 (435) 258-1278

 rockhillcheese.com

❧ 𝟕𝟔 ❧

A TRUE TASTE OF CACHE VALLEY

Get in the car and explore Cache Valley by dropping by any or all of the 20 stops on the self-guided Foodie Trek and Signature Products Tour created by the Cache Valley Visitors Bureau. Look forward to delightful chocolate, cheese, ice cream, cookies, honey, deli meats and coffee all made right here. Signature products include socks, pajamas and goats milk soap. Download the details from the Visitors Bureau website. *Our tip:* Bring a big cooler.

 199 North Main in Logan

 (435) 755-1890

 explorelogan.com

77

A FEW OF OUR
UNIQUE EATERIES

Logan has lots of great local dining spots, and here's a small sample.

Herm's Inn boasts it's the "Last chance for good food" on your way to Logan Canyon. Try the gigantic cinnamon swirl pancake with cream cheese frosting or the homestyle mac n' cheese so yummy it'll make a grown man cry (just ask Jesse).

1435 Canyon Rd. • (435) 792-4321 • hermsinn.com

Crumb Brothers Bakery is the most European bakery this side of the Continent. Do yourself a favor and try the pain au chocolat and eat it on the delightfully landscaped patio.

291 South 300 West • (435) 753-0875 • crumbbrothers.com

Le Nonne might be the most charming dining experience in Cache Valley. Our favorite Tuscan specialties created by chef Pier Antonio Micheli are chicken Milanese and salmon farfalle. Open for dinner only.

129 North 100 East • (435) 752-9577 • lenonne.com

FOOD

78

A BLUEBIRD
FOR HAPPINESS

The Bluebird Candy Company has been whipping up delightful confections since 1914. Each of their mouthwatering candies is made from scratch and their original recipes. We're pretty sure you can actually taste the love. Step inside their charming shop and watch them roll out candy centers and hand-dip chocolates. Their most popular seller is the Victoria—dark or milk chocolate with a rum-flavored center packed with chopped walnuts. One local favorite is the O'Aggie bar (named after Utah State University)—milk chocolate wrapped around caramel and brazil nuts. We recommend…well, everything.

FOOD

 75 West Center in Logan

 (435) 753-3670

 bluebirdcandy.com

SHOPPING

Middle of the Block at the Sign of the Clock

A LITTLE BIT OF
EVERYTHING

You can tell Smithfield Implement is a spunky place when they call themselves the "biggest little store in the West" and mark their closing time as 5:55 p.m. Where else can you buy a pressure cooker, fencing, cowboy hats, foil emergency blankets, a bicycle seat and a toy tractor under one roof? You get the idea. Go check it out.

 99 North Main in Smithfield

 (435) 563-3211

 smithfieldimp.com

DIAMONDS
ARE A GIRL'S BEST FRIEND

Just ask Julie because together Joe Needham integrated Jesse's ideas to design and create her eye-catching engagement and wedding rings. Joe is a brilliant and creative artist and all their work is done on site. Needham Jewelers has been a mainstay in downtown Logan since 1896 and is the oldest jewelry store in Utah. They're not just about diamonds (although you should know that Gene Needham travels to Antwerp, Belgium every year to personally select the inventory), but they have all types of precious stones and jewelry in an array of price ranges. Take time to browse the antique jewelry collection. The adjoining part of the store sells higher-end specialty gifts like Lladro figurines. Just look for the "Middle of the Block at the Sign of the Clock." You'll know it when you see it.

 141 North Main in Logan

 (435) 752-7149

 seneedham.com

81

ANOTHER MAN'S
TREASURE

Cache Valley has some great antique stores. Julie is a museum and history nerd so she loves to investigate the relics because she can touch them instead of just see them behind glass. Biggest regret for not purchasing: a French bread warming hut. How can you not die laughing at that?

Hidden Treasures
692 North 600 West in Logan • (435) 755-6022

Country Village Antique Mall
760 West 200 North in Logan • (435) 752-1678

Cache Valley Antiques
51 North Main in Logan • (435) 213-3398

Smithfield Shoppes Uptown
119 North Main in Smithfield • (435) 563-6000

82

SNOOZE IN STYLE

Sleep in heavenly peace or at least look cute when you toss and turn while wearing Lazy One pajamas. Visit the Lazy One outlet for comfortable pajamas and other clothing with creative and humorous sayings on them. Think jammies covered with moose that say, "Don't moose with me" or covered with cows that say, "I'm moo-dy in the morning." They even sell long-johns called flapjacks complete with a trapdoor in sizes all the way from infants to adults. Pick up boxer shorts, aprons (we love to wear our coordinating moose set), slippers, bibs and even pajamas for your dog. You'll see their products in resort town souvenir shops all over the country, but you can get them at a discount price here.

 3065 North 200 West in North Logan

 (435) 563-1011

 lazyone.com

83

SHOPPING
LIKE IT SHOULD BE

Shopping at the Sportsman is the kind of experience you wish you could have every time you step foot inside a store. The merchandise selection is impeccable, and the welcoming employees know every detail about every product from the way a shoe brand fits to the benefits of one sleeping bag over another. The Sportsman features technical clothing and classy sportswear as well as camping gear, skis and bikes and all the supplies that go with them. They have rentals available too.

 129 North Main in Logan

 (435) 752-0211

 thesportsmanltd.com

84

ISLAND MARKET

The Market is reminiscent of a bygone era when little stores popped up in neighborhoods to provide the basics for area residents. It's as much about the experience as purchasing the products. Here you'll find locally grown and made food products and regulars who know each other like family. It's located in an area of Logan called the "Island," which is mysterious since no one seems to know why it got its name.

 400 East Center in Logan

 (435) 752-6220

 No website

85

WORDS
AND MUCH MORE

When you walk inside the Book Table, one thing you'll notice is it smells like a book store. If you love books, that alone will give you a little burst of adrenaline. Compared to national chains, their department is fairly small, but it has a good selection including books for kids. In the past few years, they've broadened their offerings. Although it's called the *Book* Table, they have a music department with instruments, sheet music and even lessons, a toy department with fun and educational games and puzzles and scrapbooking supplies. Most of the upstairs is an Amazon outlet where they sell overstock and returned goods. You could get lost winding through shelves bursting with random products.

 29 South Main in Logan

 (435) 752-3055

 loganbooktable.wordpress.com

86

OUR LOCAL
TIFFANY'S

Deseret Industries is a secondhand store that is so huge and amazing it puts many department stores to shame. The place has been nicknamed Tiffany's by some of our seasonal residents and you won't believe the high quality of items there from clothing to antiques to collectable treasures, furniture, outdoor gear and anything else you can imagine. It's fun just to look around and see what you can find. Search for the most unique item or shop for a new outfit. Deseret Industries relies on donations from Cache Valley residents. The gleaming store is run by the Church of Jesus Christ of Latter-day Saints and serves as a way to provide goods to those in need and as a training program to help employees learn job skills so they can gain enhanced future employment.

 175 West 1400 North in Logan

 (435) 752-4511

 deseretindustries.org

SHOPPING

87

POWERFUL PATCHWORK

First of all, you should know that we don't quilt. But we do know that My Girlfriend's Quilt Shoppe was ranked as one of the Top 10 quilt shops in the nation by people who actually know what they're talking about *(Quilt Sampler Magazine)*. You can walk in without a clue and leave with new friends who don't make fun of you for thinking a fat quarter is something on your backside. Girlfriend's carries high-end, high-quality designer fabrics and they are a jackpot of supplies and ideas for any kind of project you can stitch. They have special access to all Kimberbell products (an on-fire online company that sells patterns, fabric, embroidery kits and lots more) because it just so happens the owners of Kimberbell and the Quilt Shoppe are twin sisters. Take advantage of all sorts of classes and retreats.

 1115 North 200 East #230 in Logan

 (435) 213-3229

 MyGirlfriendsQuiltShoppe.com

✦✦CELEBRATE!✦✦

Cache Valley Cruise-In

88

CUDDLE
BABY ANIMALS
OR HAVE SOME HARVEST FUN

You really can't imagine how awesome the Heritage Center is until you experience it. It gets bigger and better all the time and two prime examples are Baby Animal Days in April and the Fall Harvest Festival in October. Kids go bonkers over the chance to hold or pet baby chicks, goslings, sheep, cows, goats and pigs. Parents and grandparents are thrilled to watch the kids having so much fun. There are pony rides, train rides, wagon rides, special entertainment and all sorts of crafts and activities with pioneers, mountain men and 1900s farmers. *Tips:* Crowds are smaller on Thursday. Also, the big festival is held one week, but you can come to pet the baby animals the other weekends in April.

The most impressive thing about Fall Harvest Days is watching a giant steam engine power a thresher. Bundles of wheat are tossed in and separated. The grain goes one way and the straw gets blown out of a tall pipe into a big pile. There's also a corn maze, old-fashioned corn shelling and apple pressing and other games and activities. These events are great fun for all the generations of your family.

 4025 South Hwy. 89-91 in Wellsville

 (435) 245-6050

 awhc.org

❧ **89** ❧

WAGONS, HO!

Celebrate the arrival of the Mormon pioneers into the Salt Lake Valley on July 24, 1847. Over time, some 60,000 members of the Church of Jesus Christ of Latter-day Saints made the exodus west to escape persecution. July 24 is a state holiday. Logan and North Logan put on daylong celebrations with spirit. Now's your chance to join a watermelon or pie-eating contest. There are games, music and food, and Logan does fireworks that night. For a more authentic experience, head to the American West Heritage Center on Saturday of that week so you can participate in outdoor living history activities with costumed pioneers, visit cabins and a dugout, pull a handcart, make crafts, play games and enter contests of skill.

Logan: loganutah.org

North Logan: northlogancity.org

American West Heritage Center: awhc.org

90

COWBOY RHYME TIME

Every March the Cache Valley Cowboy Rendezvous pulls together dozens of cowboy poets and musicians for three days of fun. Many of the events are free. It's also fun to mosey past all sorts of booths containing Western goods and art and to eat some genuine Dutch oven vittles. They hold a headliner concert, workshops of all types (sometimes even harmonica!), cowboy church, a family dance, poetry contests for kids and adults and more.

 255 South 800 East in Hyrum

 No phone

 CacheValleyCowboyRendezvous.com

ॐ **91** ॐ

GOD BLESS AMERICA

There might be more patriotic passion in Logan and Cache Valley than anywhere else in America. Logan's Freedom Fire Independence Day Celebration boasts one of the largest fireworks shows in the West, partly because Fireworks West is headquartered here. They do huge shows like the opening ceremonies for the Olympics, and they're happy to show off for the locals every July 3 (why the 3rd? It's a long story). For a real thrill, pay the few bucks to get into the stadium for the music, flags and tributes. The city of Hyrum holds rodeos the week before and a patriotic program on Sunday night at the park. Hyrum and Lewiston both have a parade and usually one or more of these: a water fight with firemen, chuckwagon breakfast, baseball game, booths and entertainment, fun run, horse pulls and fireworks.

Logan: 1000 North 800 East • loganutah.org

Hyrum: Town square • hyrumcity.org

Lewiston: Town square • lewiston-ut.org

92

MEET ME AT THE FAIR

The City meets the Country at the Cache County Fair and Rodeo held the second week of August every year. We have one of the best fairs in the state, and that's not just because Julie has won blue ribbons there. It's cool to realize how much time and hard work go into raising and showing the animals, quilting, growing gigantic pumpkins, creating artwork and everything in-between. We must be city folks because until the fair we had no idea there were about a zillion varieties of chickens and rabbits. There are more than 300 commercial booths, a carnival, music and enough cotton candy for all. People watching is the best part. PRCA (professional level) rodeos are held nightly in the outdoor arena. *Tip:* If you've never tried a funnel cake, you should.

 450 South 500 West in Logan

 (435) 750-9896

 cachecounty.org/fair

93

IT'S FUR REAL

During the 1820s, strapping young mountain men hung out in Cache Valley to trap beavers. There was a big demand for the furs since the hottest fashion trend on the East Coast and in London was beaver hats and coats. They made their money and mostly held big parties when the trading companies came west with supplies and cash. All the mountain men gathered to celebrate. See a trading post and learn mountain man skills all summer long at the American West Heritage Center, but to really jump in, go to the Rendezvous, usually held in conjunction with their Pioneer Day celebration around the 24th of July. Mountain men and women are wearing leather clothing they've made and decorated by hand. There's traders' row where they sell beads and furs, decorative knives and other goods. You can try archery, tomahawk throwing and see other demonstrations like starting a fire with flint and steel.

 4025 South Hwy. 89-91 in Wellsville

 (435) 245-6050

 awhc.org

HOT WHEELS

The Cache Valley Cruise-In classic car show roars into town with around 1,000 hot rods, modified and specialty cars and motorcycles. These meticulously restored gems bring new meaning to show-and-tell. Proud owners are happy to chat all about their automotive beauties and the work that went into restoring them while you try not to drool. Music, food and automotive booths round out the offerings. Your admission ticket puts you in a drawing to win a newly restored classic car. One catch: You must be present to win. The Cruise-In is held the first Saturday in July and the Thursday and Friday before.

 450 South 500 West in Logan

 (435) 799-7149

 CacheValleyCruiseIn.com

95

GORGEOUS GOURDS
ON DISPLAY

Honestly, it's nearly impossible to describe the annual Pumpkin Walk and do it justice. You really can't imagine it until you've seen it yourself. Community groups paint, carve and even dress gourds, squash and pumpkins to create a variety of scenes according to each year's theme. The pathways of Elkridge Park are lined with carved and lit pumpkins to view while you walk past the larger scenes. It takes about 3,000 pumpkins every year! It's a favorite fall tradition held in October. Dress warmly. Just trust us and go.

 1190 East 2500 North in North Logan

 (435) 752-1310

 northlogancity.org/pumpkin-walk

96

BASH TO THE LAST

There's something exhilarating about watching the cars ram into each other at the Demolition Derby. Julie thinks maybe it's because she envisions doing the same thing to half the drivers in Logan. Whatever your reason for going, it's a wild night full of revving engines, cars crashing from all directions, steam flying up from punctured radiators and who knows what else. The derbies happen about three times during the summer along with trash car racing, another colorful car event.

 450 South 500 West in Logan

 (435) 750-9896 (fairgrounds)

 cachecounty.org/fairgrounds

97

SMALL-TOWN CELEBRATIONS

Almost every town in Cache Valley has its own reason to party and most have been happening annually for decades. It's so fun to feel such a great sense of community, even if you're just dropping in. Most have parades, games, booths, music, food and traditions unique to that town. Visit Smithfield's Health Days, Mendon's May Day (complete with dancers weaving ribbons around the May pole), Richmond's Black and White Days (the longest running festival in tribute to the Holstein cow west of the Mississippi—now that's a mouthful. Seeing the horse pulls is very impressive), Clarkston's Pony Express Days, Paradise's Trout and Berry Days, Wellsville's Founders Day and several others.

 Various towns

 No phone

 explorelogan.com (calendar)

98

BECOME A
TRUE AGGIE

Slap on some lip balm and head for Old Main Hill. The base of the hill is 500 North 700 East in Logan. Old Main is the stately building with the A on top (which stands for Aggies because Utah State was originally the Agricultural College). Climb about 1.6 million stairs and you'll be there or park on campus and save yourself from hyperventilating. The A is on the northeast side. It's blue and white and consists of a cement square resting on four A's. To become a True Aggie you must either: stand on the A and kiss someone who is already a True Aggie at midnight on a full moon, or kiss anyone you want at midnight on homecoming as long as you're in the vicinity. Since anyone can become a True Aggie that night, tons of people will be smooching up there. Only one of us is a True Aggie and without naming names, it's probably the one with messy red hair.

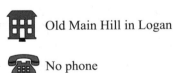 Old Main Hill in Logan

 No phone

usu.edu

99

HANG OUT IN
PARADISE

Who doesn't want to say they've been there? This tiny town is 12 miles south of Logan and holds its annual Trout and Berry Days celebration the last week of August. The festival is held because the Weeks family is one of the largest commercial growers of berries in the state (and they make delicious jams, jellies and juices) and Sportsman's Paradise hosts fly-fishermen from all over who snag beautiful trout from the local streams.

 Paradise

 (435) 245-6737

 paradise.utah.gov

✸100✸

HITCH A RIDE

Jump on one of the white and blue Cache Valley Transit District (CVTD) buses and explore our valley from top to bottom. Did we mention it's *free*? CVTD is one of the models for the best fare-free transit systems in the entire country. Get online and plot your route if you have a specific location in mind, or better yet, get on the bus and ride around its entire route. You can take 16 different trips.

 150 East 500 North in Logan

 (435) 752-2877

 cvtdbus.org

❧ **101** ❧

STRIKE!

What do you get when you cross 16 lanes of bowling with flashing lasers and loud music? Cosmic bowling at the Gutter inside the Cache Valley Fun Park. You can test your out-of-this-world skills every night (Mon.-Sat.) starting at 8 p.m. You can bowl without special effects the rest of the time. After you hit your 300 game, you can play pool, arcade games and laser tag. Trade your bowling shoes for roller skates or check out the Park Café for pizza or smoothies (and a lot of other yummy items).

 255 East 1770 North in North Logan

 (435) 792-4000

 CacheValleyFunPark.com

·❧102❧·

CATCH A FLICK

Lewiston is Cache Valley's northernmost town and probably has more cows than people. Part of the super-small-town charm is their theater. They play movies on Friday, Saturday and Monday and tickets are $2. Concessions are also $2 or less. It's a pretty cheap date. Keep your eyes open for the nondescript brown brick building that houses the city offices on one side and the theater on the other. While you're in town, you should check out the Sinclair station at 1590 West Center where you can buy a variety of candies for 2 cents each and pick up a new bicycle tire or choose from a wall full of every size of bolts you can imagine.

 2900 South Main in Lewiston

 (435) 258-1101

 lewiston-ut.org

❧ 103 ❧

SLIP AND SLIDE

If your idea of a good time is taking a flying leap down a giant water slide made out of a piece of plastic, the Redneck Water Slide is the adventure for you. If your idea of a good time is making fun of other people taking that flying leap, it's also the adventure for you. Two places provide the fun: Cherry Peak Ski Resort in Richmond—reserve it for large groups Monday through Friday with open admission on Saturday and Little Bear Bottoms in Wellsville is for groups only. The slides have steep drop-offs and you can hit speeds over 20 miles per hour so hold on to your shorts or suits or whatever you wear. You'll probably get muddy and need a chiropractor when it's all said and done, but you'll definitely have a blast.

Cherry Peak: Turn east into Richmond and follow the signs (435) 200-5050 • skicherrypeak.com

Little Bear Bottoms: 5000 South Hwy. 89/91
Reservations: (435) 770-5226

❧ 104 ❧

SNAPSHOTS
TO REMEMBER

All you have to do is open your eyes and look around wherever you are in Cache Valley and you'll find beauty and unique subjects that would make National Geographic jealous. Take a day and your camera and jaunt down any old road. Who cares if you get lost? You'll find your way back. Drink in your surroundings and enjoy the journey while you take selfies and stunning photos of whatever beauty you find. *Tip:* Your photos will be better if you avoid shooting outdoors in direct sun between 11 a.m. and 2 p.m. when the light and shadows are harsh.

 All over Cache Valley

 No phone

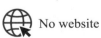 No website

RANDOM

GO AGGIES!

Utah State University students have a well-earned reputation for their rowdiness at football and basketball games. Ride the wave of adrenaline by going to one of the games. The excitement is palpable, especially for basketball in the indoor Spectrum where the screaming and cheering reverberates across the cement walls. You'll see plenty of painted faces, costumes, signs and antagonists behind the basket who love to heckle the other team. To avoid looking clueless, practice the lyrics to the century-old Scotsman, USU's fight song: *"Show me the Scotsman who doesn't love the thistle. Show me the Englishman who doesn't love the rose. Show me a true-blooded Aggie from Utah who doesn't love the spot where the sagebrush grows."* You can figure out the actions on the spot.

 1000 North 800 East in Logan (Maverik Stadium)
900 East 900 North in Logan (The Spectrum)

 (435) 797-0305

 utahstateaggies.com

❧ 106 ❧

TAKE ME OUT
TO THE BALLPARK

Plenty of Cache Valley-ites love to watch or play baseball. It's an all-American way to spend your evening. Local competitive men's teams play from May through the first week in August. Our teams are: the Providence Wolverines, Hyrum Hornets, Logan Royals and Smithfield Blue Sox. Each town has its own ball diamond where they play their home games.

 Providence, Hyrum, Logan and Smithfield

 No phone

 Search online for any of the teams season schedule

107

U-PICK

Take a short drive north to the delightful setting of Mt. Naomi farms at the base of the hills in Smithfield. The scenery is an added bonus to having the chance to pick your own ripe and delicious strawberries, grapes, blackberries and raspberries. They've got acres of them and they are lip-smackingly delicious. Check their website or give them a call to make sure the fruit is ripe.

 4460 North 400 East in Hyde Park

 (435) 232-8502

 TheVineyardsAtMtNaomiFarms.com

❧108❧

JUMP FOR JOY

Release your inner acrobat on the dozens of trampolines at the Jump Zone, an indoor park where jumpers of all ages can bounce to their heart's content. There are special jumping areas with safety nets for kids. Then there are trampolines of different heights along with soft air bags for sweet landings and extreme trampolines for all sorts of acrobatics.

 1510 North 200 West

 (435) 755-5867

 TheJumpZoneGetAir.com

𝄞109𝄞

BABY, IT'S COLD INSIDE

Tie on some ice skates and take to the sheet at the Eccles Ice Center where Olympic teams trained for the 2002 Olympics. If you're lucky, maybe their skills rubbed off on the ice. Even if they didn't, you can rent a walker to help you balance. Great news for Julie, who has no coordination and would certainly need a walker if she attempted to skate without one. The whole experience costs less than a movie. For some added screaming, crashing and possible fighting, drop in for a USU hockey game.

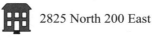 2825 North 200 East

 (435) 787-2288

 ecclesice.com

❧ **110** ❧

FLAMBOYANT FLOWERS

Spring and summer are so beautiful in Cache Valley and part of the reason is because we have so many lovely gardens. Take time to smell the roses and plenty of other blooms. You'll be impressed by:

The Temple of the Church of Jesus Christ of Latter-day Saints
175 North 300 East in Logan

Their meticulously manicured huge beds and fountains provide great photo opportunities. Although entrance to the temple is reserved for church members in good standing, the grounds are open to all.

Utah State University Campus
Stroll through campus and you'll be bombarded by exploding colorful blooms.

Logan Iris Society Show
Something about the soil and climate in Cache Valley makes magic for irises. The Society holds shows and garden tours usually around the first weekend in June and informational workshops and sales throughout the year.

BEYOND

Bear Lake, Utah

✸⚬111⚬✸

BREAK AWAY TO
BEAR LAKE

Bear Lake has been nicknamed the Caribbean of the Rockies because of its stunning turquoise water and sandy beaches. The lake is about 20 miles long and 8 miles wide and straddles Idaho and Utah. Appreciating the beautiful drive from Logan along the National Scenic Byway is part of the Bear Lake experience. If you love the water, there are a couple state parks where you can swim and play on the beach. Brace yourself because the water is always cold. You can also rent boats and watercraft for a little more action. Fishing is popular and keep your eyes peeled for the legendary Bear Lake Monster. The area is famous for its raspberries and it is almost a law that you must have a fresh raspberry shake while you're there. Also consider taking in a live show at the massively popular Pickleville Playhouse (picklevilleplayhouse.com). *Tip:* Don't miss the best view of the lake. It's at the rest stop at the summit. There are interesting informational signs, hummingbird feeders and the spectacular view. P.S. The color of the water has a lot to do with the reflection of the sky. The lake can look pretty blah on cloudy, gray days, but electric blue on clear ones.

 40 miles east of Logan

 (435) 946-3343

 bearlake.org

🎋112🎋

TOUR
MINNETONKA
CAVE

This limestone cave is a half-mile of eerie wonder. There are cream and rust-colored stalactites and stalagmites (Mom taught Julie the difference: stalac*tites* hang *tight* to the ceiling), banded travertine and formations that look like shiny, wet, melting wedding cakes. The Three Sisters formation is especially impressive and with a good imagination you can spot the cave's version of the seven dwarfs. This half-mile trek is not for the faint of heart. There are 444 stairs and you take them both ways. The cave is open from Memorial Day to Labor Day. *Tips:* Do not bring anything that has ever been inside another cave (to protect the resident bats from disease). Bring a sweatshirt or jacket and maybe gloves (for cold handrails); the cave is a not-so-balmy 40 degrees year-round. First come, first serve so you may have to wait. Cash or checks only. Call ahead to reserve a tour for 15 people or more.

 10 miles west of St. Charles, Idaho

 (435) 245-4422

 sceniccanyons.com/Minnetonka-cave

BEYOND

MADDOX
RANCH HOUSE

In our estimation, your taste buds cannot comprehend heaven until you have tasted fresh, fluffy rolls smothered with raspberry honey butter at Maddox. They're so good that locals eat as many rolls and cornbread muffins as they can and take their meals home in a box. Maddox Ranch House has been the mecca for their skinless fried chicken since 1949. Don't shy away from trying their turkey steak. It's breaded ground turkey breast…hard to describe but definitely delicious. If you've ever wanted to try buffalo, sink your teeth into one of their bison steaks or burgers. And please, oh please, save room for dessert. The seasonal pies are made from fresh fruit grown in the surrounding orchards. *Tip:* The place is always busy and with good reason. We suggest making a reservation no matter what time you go. If you'd like a more casual experience, pull into the adjacent old-fashioned drive-in. Closed Sundays and Mondays.

 1900 South Hwy. 89 in Perry

 (800) 544-5474

 maddoxfinefood.com

BEYOND

❧114❧

PETTINGILL'S
AND THE FAMOUS
FRUITWAY

Mother Nature has smiled on Box Elder County 19 miles west of Logan where the farmers have mastered the art of growing about every variety of vegetable and fruit (except citrus). Brigham City marks the northernmost border of the 2-mile stretch of Hwy. 89 known as the Famous Fruitway. Meander past more than a dozen family-owned fruit stands through the communities of Perry and Willard. They all sell glorious produce, but we don't stop until we get to Pettingill's, the very last one. Pettingills are third-generation orchardists and denim overall-clad Grandpa Gay started the business by selling peaches out of a wagon when he was a kid. Now the bustling stand sells berries, cherries, apricots, apples, pears, melons and 42 varieties of peaches. Then there are the beautiful baskets of bright red tomatoes, cucumbers, corn and onions and that's only scratching the surface. You'll catch customers thumping the watermelons and smelling the cantaloupe, but it's really not necessary since all the produce is ripened to perfection and arrives daily straight from area fields. *Tip:* Pettingills also has a shake shack where they mix fruit (they get it straight from their stand) with locally made hard ice cream for a bite of fruity, frosty heaven. They are huge, so plan on sharing or getting a brain freeze headache if you conquer one on your own.

8815 Hwy. 89 in Willard • (801) 782-8001

❧ **115** ❧

GOLDEN SPIKE
NATIONAL HISTORIC SITE

East met West May 10, 1869, when the Southern Pacific and the Union Pacific railroads joined the nation with the completion of the first transcontinental railroad at Promontory Point, west of Brigham City. The golden spike was the final railroad spike driven into the wooden railroad ties at the wedding of the rails ceremony. In the iconic photo, the Central Pacific and Union Pacific engines sit nose to nose while the company VIPs celebrate with champagne and everyone else in the foreground looks cranky. The national historic site runs full-size replica steam engines of *Jupiter* and *No. 119* daily from May 1 through mid-October. Volunteers re-create the final ceremony on Saturdays during those months. It's quite impressive. There is also an auto tour where you can see the railroad's cuts, fills and culverts. *Tips:* Fill up with gas and snacks because there are no services at Promontory. Bring water bottles, sunscreen and bug repellant. Follow the signs and not your GPS.

 I-15 north to exit 365. Turn west on UT Hwy. 13/83 for 32 miles

 (435) 471-2209

 nps.gov/gosp

BEYOND

SPREAD YOUR WINGS

Remember when you were little and you used Crayons to draw pictures of birds that all looked like a brown letter V? Plenty of folks still think that's about the extent of bird species besides an occasional ostrich, turkey, eagle or parrot. At the Bear River Migratory Bird Refuge, you'll open your eyes when you see samplings of more than 270 varieties. The refuge is on a major migration route, so a larger-than-usual array are passing through. The refuge is 80,000 acres of unspoiled nature with several habitats and they have designed a one-way, 12-mile auto loop that allows you to explore the habitats and see the birds and wildlife without even leaving your car. Look for some of their "priority birds": pelicans, snowy plovers, black-necked stilts and cinnamon teals. Get into nature by taking the 1.5-mile boardwalk path through wetlands right outside the Wildlife Education Center, which is open Tuesdays-Fridays and the 2nd and 4th Saturday. The auto loop is open every day. *Tips:* If you are not a bird nerd already, stop by the Visitors Bureau in Logan to pick up a pocket birding guide for quick and easy identification. Also, get your hands on some binoculars if you possibly can.

 I-15 exit 363, just north of Brigham City

 (435) 723-8873

 fws.gov (search for Bear River)

❧117❧

PAY TRIBUTE TO THE
SLAIN SHOSHONE

In the 1860s tension had been escalating between the native
Shoshone Indians and the region's settlers. There were misdeeds
on both parts, but many of the settlers' reports were blown out of
proportion. U.S. Army Colonel Patrick Connor and his soldiers
were deployed to Utah to keep the peace. Connor took matters
into his own hands and in the early morning hours on January
29, 1863, he and his soldiers attacked a Shoshone settlement and
slaughtered approximately 400 men, women and children in the
Bear River Massacre, the largest massacre in American history.
It's interesting to read the white people's perspective of the events
on a marker placed at the national historic site years ago. The
location is serene. You may notice pouches or other items hanging
from the branches of a nearby tree. These items are sacred to the
Shoshone and can represent prayers and requests for assistance
from deity. A new welcome interpretive center is underway.

BEYOND

 2945 Hwy. 91, northwest of Preston, Idaho

 No phone

 nwbShoshone.com/culture

The opinions and suggestions in this book are solely ours. There is no endorsement made or implied by the Cache Valley Visitors Bureau or by any of the subjects in the featured entries.

Notes

Notes

Notes

Notes

117 AMAZING THINGS TO DO IN LOGAN AND CACHE VALLEY UTAH

Jesse and Julie Hollist Terrill

Printed in the United States of America

First Printing, 2018